MIND YOUR OWN MIND

MASTER FOCUS, BUILD RESILIENCE, EMBRACE PRESENT-MOMENT AWARENESS, AND TRANSFORM TO A WINNING MINDSET

ABILASHA U R

Mind your own Mind (The Journey Towards Inner Peace)

"Mind your own mind" is a phrase often used to remind someone to focus on their own thoughts, feelings, and actions rather than meddling in or worrying about the thoughts and actions of others.

It suggests a sense of self-awareness and mindfulness, encouraging individuals to prioritize their own mental well-being and personal growth.

DEDICATION AND ACKNOWLEDGMENTS

To all those who strive for inner peace and embrace the journey of self-discovery.

I am deeply grateful to everyone who has contributed to the realization of this book. To my family and friends, your unwavering support and encouragement have been my guiding light. To my mentors and teachers, thank you for sharing your wisdom and inspiring my journey of mindfulness and personal growth. And to you, dear readers, your openness to explore these teachings fuels my passion for spreading mindfulness.

May this book serve as a beacon of mindfulness and empowerment for all who seek clarity and peace in their lives.

FOREWORD

If you've ever wondered about the inner workings of your mind, how to navigate life's challenges with clarity, or find peace amidst chaos, then "Mind Your Own Mind" by Abhilasha is your essential companion. This book explores the complexities of human psychology, drawing on insights from mindfulness practices and psychology to help you reclaim control over your thoughts and emotions.

As a Mind Performance Coach and the author of the bestseller "Unleash the Power of Reading," I understands how self-awareness and personal growth can transform lives. In a world filled with distractions and challenges, do you find it difficult to maintain clarity? "Mind Your Own Mind" offers insights to help you regain control of your thoughts and emotions.

In today's fast-paced world, external pressures and internal struggles often cloud our clarity. "Mind Your Own Mind" serves as a guiding light to reclaim ownership of your thoughts and emotions. This journey isn't about withdrawing from the world but about understanding your motivations and values, and learning to navigate life with clarity, purpose, and peace.

Throughout the book, practical strategies and insights from psychology and mindfulness practices are shared, offering tools to cultivate a growth mindset, set healthy boundaries, and embrace mindfulness. These tools empower you to filter out external noise and create a life that aligns with your true self.

Whether you're feeling overwhelmed by societal pressures, wrestling with self-doubt, or simply seeking a deeper sense of self-awareness, "Mind Your Own Mind" is here to support you. If you're ready to cultivate a growth mindset, set healthy boundaries, and embrace mindfulness, "Mind Your Own Mind" is your essential companion. It's a transformative read that promises to illuminate the path to a happier, healthier, and more fulfilling life.

Best Wishes,

(Dr. Manjunath M.S.)
Mind Performance Coach and Author of "Unleash the Power of Reading"

Preface

Welcome to "**Mind Your Own Mind**"! As you hold this book in your hands, you might be wondering what lies within these pages and why I chose to write it.

The idea behind this book came from journey of exploring the complexities of the human mind. In today's fast-paced, challenging world, we often find ourselves overwhelmed by external influences, societal pressures, and internal struggles. "Mind Your Own Mind" is an invitation to reclaim ownership of our thoughts, emotions, and mental well-being. We'll delve into the reasons why we get caught up in the external world, and how this constant noise can drown out our inner voice.

This journey is not about becoming isolated or self-absorbed. Instead, it's about **claiming your inner power** by understanding your motivations, values, and desires. It's about learning to navigate the world with **clarity, purpose, and peace**.

"Mind Your Own Mind" is your guide to **cultivating a growth mindset, setting healthy boundaries, and embracing mindfulness**. With these tools, you'll learn to **filter out the external noise** and create a life that truly aligns with who you are.

Whether you're feeling overwhelmed by societal pressures, struggling with self-doubt, or simply learning for a deeper sense of self-awareness, this book is here to support you. Join me as we embark on a journey to **rediscover the power and beauty of your own mind**.

Throughout these chapters, I included some practical strategies and insights drawn from psychology, mindfulness practices, and personal experiences. My goal is not to provide a quick-fix solution but rather to empower you with the tools needed to cultivate a healthier relationship with your mind.

I want to express my deepest gratitude to everyone who supported me throughout the creation of this book—my family, friends, and mentors who provided encouragement and inspiration along the way. Additionally, I extend my appreciation to the readers who embark on this journey with an open mind and a willingness to explore new perspectives.

Whether you're seeking clarity amidst chaos, striving for personal growth, or simply curious about the workings of the mind, I hope this book serves as a beacon of guidance and inspiration.

Remember, the **journey of self-discovery** begins with the decision to "Mind Your Own Mind."

Thank you for joining me on this adventure of understanding and embracing the power of our own mind.

Warm regards,
Abilasha U R

CONTENTS

INTRODUCTION

Welcome to "**Mind Your Own Mind: Embracing Present-Moment Awareness.**"

In a world filled with constant distractions, demands, and uncertainties, it's easy to lose sight of what truly matters—**the present moment**. Our minds always think on the past or worrying about the future, leaving us feeling disconnected and overwhelmed with the present moment.

Present moment awareness, also called mindfulness, is a practice to focusing our attention to **"NOW"**

"Mind Your Own Mind" is an invitation to reclaim control of your mental landscape. Here, we embark on a journey of **self-discovery** that emphasizes the importance of **focusing on your own thoughts, beliefs, and mental well-being**. This isn't about becoming isolated; it's about cultivating **clarity, purpose, and inner peace** amidst the external noise.

This book delves into the reasons why we get caught up in the external world, exploring the psychological mechanisms that drive our need for approval and fear of missing out. We'll equip you with practical tools for:

- Developing a growth mindset: Embrace the power of learning and continuous improvement.

- Practicing mindfulness: Become more present and aware of your thoughts and emotions.

- Setting healthy boundaries: Protect your mental energy by establishing clear limits.

- Quieting the inner critic: Learn to silence negative self-talk that holds you back.

Imagine Sarah, a busy professional juggling a demanding job, family responsibilities, and social commitments. Each day, she finds herself caught up in a whirlwind of activity, constantly multitasking and trying to stay ahead of her endless to-do list. Despite her best efforts, Sarah often feels stressed and frazzled, unable to fully enjoy the moments as they pass by. She finds herself dwelling on past mistakes or worrying about what tomorrow may bring, rather than fully immersing herself in the beauty of the present moment.

Mindfulness practices could help Sarah become more aware of her thoughts and emotions. By focusing on the present moment, she could learn to appreciate the simple joys in life, like spending quality time with family or enjoying a quiet cup of coffee in the morning. Mindfulness can also help Sarah manage stress by teaching her techniques to calm her mind and body.

Sarah's experience mirrors that of many individuals living in our fast-paced world, where distractions abound, and the pressures of daily life can pull us away from the richness of the present moment. This sets the stage for the exploration of the central theme of this book: **the importance of present-moment awareness in finding inner peace and fulfillment.**

The phrase "**Mind Your Own Mind**" explains the essence of our life journey. It's not just about offering advice; it's an invitation to embark on a profound exploration of self-discovery and mindfulness. Through prioritizing inner reflection and self-awareness, we can achieve greater mental well-being and personal growth.

Throughout the chapters of this book, we will delve into key themes such as self-reflection, non-judgment, and impermanence—essential aspects of mindfulness and present-moment awareness. These practices have transformative potential, fostering greater connection, authenticity, and resilience in our lives.

This journey is not about striving for perfection or avoiding life's challenges. Instead, it's about embracing our humanity—including our imperfections and vulnerabilities—and finding peace and fulfillment amidst life's ups and downs.

As we explore the transformative power of present-moment awareness, we'll offer practical insights and exercises to guide you on your path. From understanding the nature of your own mind to cultivating compassion for yourself and others, each chapter is an invitation to dive deeper into the essence of mindful living.

But this journey is not just about finding peace within ourselves; it's also about recognizing our interconnectedness with the world around us. As we learn to mind our own minds, we become more attuned to the needs and experiences of others, fostering empathy and understanding that transcends boundaries.

Let us embark on this journey together—a journey of self-discovery, growth, and profound transformation. Let us learn to embrace the present moment with open hearts and open minds, knowing that within its depths lies the key to true liberation and lasting happiness.

CHAPTER 1

UNDERSTANDING THE POWER OF MINDFULNESS

"Mindfulness is the miracle by which we master and restore ourselves." – **Thich Nhat Hanh**

This chapter serves as an invitation to embark on a transformative journey – a journey inward. Here, we'll delve into the concept of mindfulness, a potent tool for mastering your mental landscape. We'll explore its essence, the power it holds, and how it can empower you to navigate the complexities of your mind.

What is Mindfulness?

Mindfulness is a transformative practice that holds the key to unlocking inner peace, resilience, and profound self-awareness. It's the practice of paying attention, on purpose, in the present moment, without judgment. It's about cultivating a heightened awareness of your thoughts, feelings, and bodily sensations – essentially, being fully present in the here and now.

Imagine your mind as a busy marketplace filled with fleeting thoughts. Mindfulness equips you to observe this marketplace with a gentle curiosity, without getting swept away by the commotion.

Presence in the Present Moment

The essence of mindfulness lies in the ability to be fully present in the here and now. Often, our minds are preoccupied with regrets from the past or anxieties about the future, causing us to miss out on the richness of the present moment. Mindfulness invites us to step out of the cycle of mental chatter and immerse ourselves in the present with open awareness.

The Power Within

Our minds are incredibly powerful. They can be a source of creativity, focus, and joy. However, they can also be prone to negativity, anxiety, and rumination.

Mindfulness offers a solution. By training your attention, you can:

- **Reduce stress and anxiety:** Mindfulness helps you detach from the whirlwind of thoughts that often fuel these emotions.

- **Enhance focus and concentration:** By anchoring yourself in the present, you become less susceptible to distractions.

- **Improve emotional regulation:** Mindfulness allows you to observe your emotions without judgment, fostering a more balanced response.

- **Boost self-awareness:** As you become more mindful, you gain a deeper understanding of your thoughts, feelings, and motivations.

- **Increase compassion:** Mindfulness fosters a sense of kindness towards yourself and others.

The Science Behind It

Research shows that mindfulness practices can have a significant impact on the brain. Studies have revealed positive changes in brain regions associated with focus, emotional regulation, and self-awareness. Mindfulness isn't just a feel-good practice; it has the potential to reshape your neural pathways for the better.

Getting Started with Mindfulness

The beauty of mindfulness is its simplicity. It doesn't require fancy equipment or memberships. Here are some ways to begin:

Cultivating Calm: Practical Ways to Practice Mindfulness

Mindfulness, the practice of focusing on the present moment without judgment, might sound simple, but putting it into practice can be a challenge. Here are some practical ways you can integrate mindfulness into your daily life, no matter how busy you are:

1. Mindful Breathing: This is the foundation of mindfulness practice. Find a quiet place, sit comfortably, and close your eyes (if that feels comfortable). Focus on your breath, feeling the rise and fall of your chest or abdomen with each inhalation and exhalation. When your mind wanders (and it will!), gently bring your attention back to your breath. Start with just a few minutes a day and gradually increase the duration as you become more comfortable.

2. Mindful Movement: You don't need to dedicate hours to meditation to be mindful. Integrate mindfulness into everyday activities like walking. As you walk, pay attention to the sensations in your body – the feel of your feet hitting the ground, the movement of your arms. Notice the sights and sounds around you

– the rustling leaves, the chirping birds. This simple practice can transform mundane tasks into opportunities for mindfulness.

3. Mindful Eating: How often do you eat mindlessly while watching TV or scrolling through your phone? Take a break from technology and savor your food mindfully. Before you begin eating, take a few moments to appreciate the colors, textures, and aromas of your food. Chew slowly, noticing the taste with each bite. This practice helps you appreciate your food and allows your body to better absorb nutrients.

4. The Mindful Body Scan: Lie down comfortably or sit in a chair. Close your eyes (optional) and take a few deep breaths. Mentally scan your body, starting from your toes and gradually moving upwards. Notice any physical sensations – tightness, relaxation, warmth, coolness. Don't judge any sensations, simply observe them with a sense of curiosity. This practice can help you release physical tension and cultivate a sense of peace within your body.

5. The 5-Minute Mindfulness Break: Feeling overwhelmed throughout the day? Take a 5-minute mindfulness break. Stand up, step away from your desk, and find a quiet spot. Take a few deep breaths, focusing on the sensation of your breath in your nostrils. Look around you and notice five things you haven't paid attention to before – a unique pattern on the wall, a spider web in the corner, the warmth of the sun on your skin. This short break can help you refocus and return to your work feeling refreshed.

6. The Mindful Moment: Throughout the day, take small moments to be mindful. As you wash your hands, feel the coolness of the water on your skin, the scent of the soap. When you answer the phone, take a deep breath before speaking, allowing yourself to be fully present in the conversation. These "micro-moments" of mindfulness can add up to a significant impact on your overall well-being.

7. Mindful Listening: In our fast-paced world, true listening is a rare commodity. When someone is talking to you, make a conscious effort to be present. Put away your phone, make eye contact, and focus on what they are saying. Ask clarifying questions and avoid interrupting. This mindful approach fosters deeper connections with others.

8. The "Mindful Technology" Paradox: While technology can be a source of distraction, it can also be a tool for mindfulness. There are many mindfulness apps available that offer guided meditations, soothing soundscapes, and reminders to practice mindfulness throughout the day. Explore these resources and find ones that resonate with you.

Consider real-life examples of how mindfulness has benefited.

1. **The Rushed Morning:** Imagine waking up late for work. Your mind races with worry – the traffic, the upcoming presentation. Instead of succumbing to panic, take a few mindful breaths. Feel your feet on the floor, the

coolness of the air. Acknowledge your anxieties, but don't let them control you. Focus on getting dressed mindfully, one step at a time. This can help you approach the day with a calmer and more collected mind.

2. **The Frustrating Commute:** Stuck in rush hour traffic? This is a perfect opportunity to practice mindful observation. Notice the different cars, the way the sunlight filters through the trees, the music playing on the radio. By focusing on these external details, you detach from the frustration of the situation.

3. **The Mindful Meeting:** During a stressful meeting, you feel your anger rising as a colleague presents a flawed idea. Instead of reacting impulsively, take a mindful breath. Observe your physical sensations – is your jaw clenched? Are your fists tight? Acknowledge your anger without judgment. Then, choose your words thoughtfully before speaking. This allows for a more productive and respectful discussion.

4. **The Mindful Meal:** How often do you eat lunch while glued to your phone or computer? Take a break from technology and savor your meal mindfully. Notice the colors of your food, the different textures, the taste with each bite. Chew slowly and appreciate the nourishment your body is receiving.

5. **The Mindful Walk:** Take a walk during your break and

truly immerse yourself in the experience. Feel the ground beneath your feet, the breeze on your skin. Listen to the sounds around you – birds chirping, leaves rustling. This simple practice can be surprisingly grounding and help you return to work feeling refreshed.

Mindfulness Practices Beyond Meditation:

While meditation is a popular mindfulness practice, it's not the only way to cultivate present-moment awareness. Here are a few additional practices you can explore:

- Mindful Movement: Activities like yoga, tai chi, or even mindful walking can be powerful tools for mindfulness. As you move your body, focus on the sensations you experience – the stretch of your muscles, the feel of your breath, the rhythm of your steps. This practice combines physical movement with present-moment awareness.

- Mindful Journaling: Take time each day to write down your thoughts and feelings without judgment. This allows you to observe your inner world with greater clarity and gain insights into your patterns and emotions.

- Mindful Creativity: Engage in activities like mindful drawing, coloring, or playing music. Let go of expectations and focus on the present experience of creating. Notice the colors, textures, and sounds involved.

These are just a few examples, and the possibilities are endless. Find what resonates with you and allows you to connect with the present moment in a meaningful way.

Common Challenges and Overcoming Them:

Wandering Mind: It's natural for your mind to wander during mindfulness practice. Don't get discouraged! When this happens, gently acknowledge the distraction, and bring your attention back to your breath or the present moment sensation.

Feeling Restless: If you find stillness challenging, start with shorter mindfulness practices and gradually increase the duration. You can also incorporate movement-based practices like mindful walking or mindful yoga.

Difficulty Focusing: If focusing on your breath feels difficult, try focusing on external sounds or sensations. Notice the sounds around you, the feel of your clothes on your skin, or the temperature in the room.

Lack of Time: Mindfulness doesn't require long stretches of time. Even a few minutes of mindful breathing or mindful eating can make a difference. Integrate brief mindfulness practices throughout your day for a cumulative impact.

Remember: Consistency is key! Don't get discouraged if your mind wanders during your practice. The goal is not to achieve a state of perfect focus, but to gently guide your attention back to the present moment. With regular practice, mindfulness will become a natural part of your life, allowing you to experience greater calm, clarity, and well-being.

Conclusion

Mindfulness is a powerful tool for cultivating self-awareness, reducing stress, and fostering inner peace. As you embark on this journey, embrace the present moment, and witness the transformative power of "minding your own mind."

CHAPTER 2

THE ART OF SELF-REFLECTION: NAVIGATING INNER DIALOGUE

"Knowing yourself is the beginning of all wisdom."
– Aristotle

Chapter 1 introduced you to mindfulness, a powerful tool for understanding your present experience. Now, we'll delve into the art of self-reflection, a practice that complements mindfulness by helping you explore your inner world – your thoughts, feelings, and experiences – to gain a deeper understanding of yourself.

Why Self-Reflection Matters

Imagine yourself lost in a crowded city. Without a map (self-reflection) and a sense of direction (mindfulness), it's easy to get overwhelmed and frustrated. Self-reflection equips you with the tools to navigate your inner city,

This helps you to:

Boost Self-Awareness: Have you ever blurted something out and later regretted it? Self-reflection allows you to identify patterns in your behavior. For example, perhaps you notice a tendency to speak impulsively when you're feeling stressed. This awareness is the first step towards managing your stress response and communicating more effectively.

Improve Emotional Regulation: Let's say you get flustered during work presentations, and your mind goes blank. Self-reflection helps you recognize the triggers for your emotions (anxiety in this case) and develop healthy coping mechanisms. By reflecting on past presentations and the emotions they elicited, you can develop calming techniques like deep breathing or visualization to use before your next one.

Make Better Decisions: Imagine a friend asks you to join them on a weekend getaway, but you have a big deadline looming. Self-reflection allows you to clarify your values and priorities. Is spending time with friends important to you? Can you delegate some work to meet your deadline? By reflecting on your priorities, you can make a decision aligned with what truly matters to you.

Embrace Personal Growth: Let's say you receive critical feedback on a project. Self-reflection isn't about dwelling on the criticism. It's about acknowledging it and using it as a springboard for growth. By identifying areas for improvement in your work, you can set goals and learn new skills to become a more well-rounded professional.

Cultivating a Self-Reflective Practice

Self-reflection doesn't have to be a time-consuming chore. Here are some practical ways to weave it into your daily life, using scenarios you might encounter:

Journaling Prompts:

Instead of staring at a blank page, use prompts to spark self-reflection. Here's an example:

Scenario: You had a disagreement with your partner. Reflecting on the situation, you write: "Today, I argued with my partner about finances. I felt frustrated and unheard. What could I have done differently to communicate my needs more effectively?"

Mindful Moments:

Throughout your day, take a "mini-pause." Notice your breath, your posture, and any emotions that might be present. Ask yourself: "What's going on for me right now?"

Scenario: You're stuck in rush hour traffic. Feeling your frustration rising, you take a mindful pause. You notice your clenched jaw and shallow breathing. Recognizing your physical signs of stress, you take a few deep breaths to calm yourself down.

Gratitude Practice:

Before sleep, take a few minutes to reflect on three things you're grateful for, big or small. This simple act can shift your focus to the positive and boost overall well-being.

Scenario: You're feeling overwhelmed by work deadlines. Take a moment to reflect. You're grateful for your job that allows you to support yourself, for your good health that allows you to work hard, and for your supportive family who motivates you.

Weekly Review:

Dedicate 15-20 minutes each week to review your past week. What were your wins? What challenges did you face? What did you learn?

<u>Scenario</u>: Reflecting on your week, you realize you aced that presentation you were nervous about (win!). You also acknowledge procrastinating on another project (challenge). Learning from this, you decide to schedule dedicated work time each day to avoid last-minute scrambling.

Seeking Feedback:

Don't be afraid to ask trusted friends, mentors, or even a therapist for feedback. Their insights can offer a fresh perspective and highlight areas for growth you might have missed.

<u>Scenario</u>: You're unsure why you keep getting passed over for promotions. Talking to a trusted colleague, you learn that your communication style can sometimes come across as overly critical. By seeking feedback, you can identify areas for improvement in your interpersonal skills.

Navigating Your Inner Dialogue

Our inner voice is a constant companion, shaping our perceptions and influencing our actions. However, this inner voice can sometimes be critical, negative, or misleading.

Self-reflection helps you become aware of your inner dialogue and distinguish helpful self-talk from unhelpful patterns. Here are some strategies to cultivate a more positive inner critic:

Challenge Negative Thoughts: Don't accept negative self-talk at face value. When a negative thought arises, question its validity. Is it based on facts, or is it distorted thinking?

Practice Self-Compassion: Treat yourself with the same kindness and understanding you would offer a friend. Acknowledge your mistakes, but don't dwell on them.

Reframe Negative Thoughts: Instead of dwelling on what went wrong, reframe the situation as a learning opportunity. How can you grow from this experience?

Replace Negative Self-Talk with Affirmations: Counteract negative thoughts with positive affirmations. Remind yourself of your strengths and capabilities.

By cultivating a self-reflective practice and navigating your inner dialogue with awareness and compassion, you can embark on a transformative journey of self-discovery and personal growth.

Chapter 3

THE MONKEY MIND - TAMING THE RESTLESS CHATTER

"Your mind is your instrument. Learn to be its master and not its slave." – **Remez Sasson**

Have you ever sat down to work on a task, only to find yourself ten minutes later scrolling mindlessly through social media? Or maybe you lie in bed at night, replaying past conversations and worrying about the future. This constant mental chatter is often referred to as the "monkey mind," a metaphor for a restless and uncontrolled mind that jumps from thought to thought like a mischievous monkey swinging from vine to vine.

Our brains are like powerful computers constantly processing information. Scientists have identified a brain network called the default mode network (DMN) that becomes active when our minds wander. This is where the "monkey business" happens. While some degree of mind-wandering is normal, a runaway monkey mind can take it to an extreme.

The incessant chatter of the monkey mind can profoundly affect our daily experiences. When our thoughts are scattered and chaotic, it becomes challenging to stay present and fully engage with the tasks at hand. We might find ourselves easily distracted, unable to focus, or overwhelmed by the sheer volume of mental noise.

Our thoughts have a direct impact on our emotions. The monkey mind can fuel feelings of anxiety, stress, and discontent by incessantly dwelling on negative scenarios or perceived threats. It can also rob us of the joy of the present moment, as we become preoccupied with regrets from the past or anxieties about the future.

Disadvantages of the Monkey Mind:

Negativity Bias: Our brains are naturally more attuned to negative thoughts than positive ones. The monkey mind amplifies this negativity, making us dwell on problems and overlook the good. Imagine a news feed filled with negativity; the monkey mind keeps refreshing it, making us feel overwhelmed by the bad news.

Rumination: We ruminate when we get stuck replaying negative experiences or worries in our minds. This can lead to anxiety, depression, and difficulty focusing on the present. The monkey mind becomes a broken record, replaying the same worries over and over again.

Impulsivity: The monkey mind can make us act without thinking clearly, leading to rash decisions and regretted actions. It's like the monkey sees a shiny distraction (like that notification) and impulsively clicks on it, forgetting the important task at hand.

Procrastination: Faced with a daunting task, the monkey mind might tempt us to avoid it altogether with distractions. The monkey might suggest all sorts of "urgent" but unimportant tasks to avoid the real work we need to do.

However, it's important to note that the human mind isn't just a "monkey mind." We have the capacity for:

1. **Mindfulness**: Despite the restless nature of the monkey mind, it is possible to find moments of stillness and clarity. By cultivating awareness through mindfulness practices, we can observe our thoughts without getting entangled in them. This awareness empowers us to respond consciously rather than react impulsively to the ebb and flow of mental activity. Practices like meditation can help us become aware of our thoughts and emotions without judgment, promoting focus and calmness.

2. **Intentional Focus:** While our minds possess an inherent tendency towards a scattered, "monkey mind" state, research demonstrates the remarkable capacity for cultivating intentional focus. This section explores evidence-based techniques to quiet internal chatter and achieve a state of concentrated attention, optimizing performance in learning, creativity, and various cognitive tasks.

Through training and effort, we can develop the ability to concentrate on the task at hand and quiet the internal chatter.

Focus: A Continuous Process

It's important to acknowledge that maintaining focus is a continual process. Don't be discouraged by initial instances of a wandering mind. This is a natural tendency. The key lies in gently refocusing your attention on the task at hand without judgment. Celebrate your progress, no matter how small, as you gradually strengthen your focus muscle. Through consistent practice and the implementation of these strategies, you can train your mind to achieve a state of laser focus, unlocking a new level of mental clarity, productivity, and overall well-being.

1. **Positive Self-Talk**: Learning to replace negative thoughts with positive affirmations can improve our mental well-being and outlook.

2. **Taking Control of the Jungle Gym:** While the monkey

mind can be a nuisance, it doesn't have to be the boss. The following chapters will explore techniques to tame the monkey mind and cultivate a more focused and peaceful inner state.

Embracing the Journey

In this journey of exploring the monkey mind, we embark on a path of self-discovery and inner exploration. We seek to understand the patterns and tendencies of our thoughts, uncovering the underlying motivations behind our actions, and ultimately reclaiming a sense of inner peace amidst the ceaseless movement of the mind.

CHAPTER 4

LETTING GO OF DISTRACTIONS: CULTIVATING MENTAL CLARITY

"Letting go of distractions unlocks mental clarity.
Focused stillness reveals our minds' true power."
– Abilasha U R

In the previous chapters, we explored the power of mindfulness, self-reflection and restless chatter of monkey mind. Now, let's delve into the art of cultivating mental clarity—the ability to focus your attention and achieve a state of mental calmness, amidst the distractions of our fast-paced world.

Letting go of distractions is the first step to cultivating mental clarity; in the stillness of focus, we find the true power of our minds.

Understanding Distractions

In today's digital age, distractions are ubiquitous. From incessant social media notifications to the constant ping of emails, our attention is constantly pulled in multiple directions. These distractions can fragment our focus, diminish productivity, and contribute to feelings of overwhelm and stress.

Imagine you're at work, trying to complete an important project. As you sit down to concentrate, your phone buzzes with a notification. Curious, you check the notification, only to be drawn into a rabbit hole of social media updates and news articles. By the time you return to your task, precious time has been lost, and your focus is disrupted.

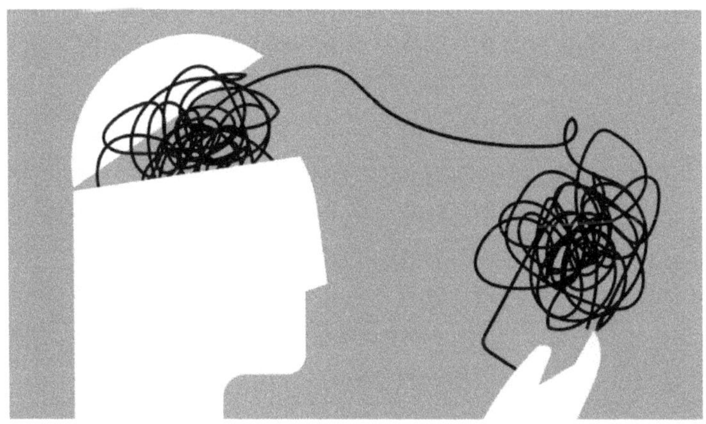

Distractions in our modern world come in many forms, and they can significantly impact our ability to maintain focus and mental clarity. It's important to recognize the types of distractions we encounter daily:

Digital Distractions: Let's be honest, alerts are nothing more than simple distractions to take you away from the task at hand. So why not just get rid of them? The constant notifications from smartphones, social media platforms, emails, and other digital devices can be highly disruptive. The allure of checking messages or scrolling through news feeds can pull us away from important tasks.

Example: Sarah is working on a project deadline when her phone chimes with a new message notification. Despite her initial intention to ignore it, she finds herself reaching for her phone and getting drawn into a lengthy conversation, losing track of time, work and focus.

How to deal with digital distractions to improve focus:

We live in a time where digital distraction is everywhere. We have access to nearly anything and everything we could ever ask for. But we need to ask ourselves: Is this a good thing?

If you're planning a honeymoon or looking for ways to build your next business, or searching to improve your physical fitness, having an endless portal of information is worth its weight in gold. But if you're like most individuals throughout the world, the internet has become a source of ongoing anxiety, stress, and fear-mongering—a digital distraction that can have devastating effects on our mental and emotional well-being.

With social media, some people want us to see their posts, photos and their content, not what they truly are at all hours during the day.

Even with the recent advancements in technology over the last few decades, our brains haven't changed much. The latest estimates suggest that our modern-day brains haven't changed in over 40,000 years, which is a blink of an eye on the trajectory of life on our planet as we know it.

As a result of this lack of change, our brains haven't been able to adapt to digital distractions—this rapidly changing technology and fast-paced lifestyle—which was created to hijack our brain's neural circuitry by creating continuous stressors that have devastating effects on our overall health.

In his infamous book, Why Zebra's Don't Get Ulcers, author Robert Sapolsky documents how stress affects both animals and humans. He essentially makes the analogy that stress isn't bad in small quantities but repeated and chronic stressors over days, weeks, months, and even years can have detrimental effects on our health. And these stressors don't even have to be real!

What does that mean? It means that perceived stress from anxiety, judgment, fear of missing out, and feelings of being inferior to others based on comparisons and social media profiles can have similar effects on our health.

This is because the brain cannot truly tell the difference between a real or perceived threat. Thus, technological advancements rarely come without a hidden cost to the people using them. So how do we battle these invisible enemies and gain back control in our lives to improve focus and enhance productivity?

To start, there's a simple question you need to ask yourself. Do you actually need to know when someone likes a friend's page? In the grand scheme of things, how impactful is it to see that you got 20 likes on your post from yesterday? And is it going to change your career trajectory if your friend posted a cat video on their TikTok/Instagram page?

Environmental Distractions: Noise, clutter, and interruptions in our physical environment can also contribute to distractions. Whether it's background chatter in a busy office, clutter on our desks, or frequent interruptions from colleagues or family members, environmental distractions can disrupt our concentration.

Example: John is trying to concentrate on reading a report in a noisy coffee shop. The constant hum of conversations and clattering of dishes makes it difficult for him to focus, leading to frustration and reduced productivity.

Internal Distractions: Our own thoughts and emotions can become distractions if they are not managed effectively. Worries, anxieties, or daydreams can hijack our attention and lead us away from the task at hand.

Example: Emily is studying for an exam but keeps thinking about a recent argument with a friend. Her mind keeps revisiting the conversation, making it challenging for her to concentrate on her study material.

Multitasking: The misconception that multitasking is efficient can actually be a major distraction. Trying to juggle multiple tasks simultaneously can lead to decreased performance and increased mental fatigue.

Example: Lisa is attempting to respond to emails, prepare a presentation, and listen to a conference call all at once. As a result, she ends up making mistakes in her emails, missing important points during the call, and feeling overwhelmed.

By understanding the various forms of distractions, we encounter, we can begin to address them more effectively and cultivate strategies to minimize their impact on our focus and mental clarity.

In the next section, we will explore practical strategies and examples for letting go of distractions and cultivating mental clarity in our daily lives.

Cultivating Mental Clarity

Cultivating mental clarity is about training your mind to let go of distractions and sharpen your focus. It involves adopting practices that promote concentration, calmness, and presence amidst the noise of modern life.

Practical Strategies for Letting Go of Distractions

Mindful Task Management: Break tasks into smaller, manageable chunks and prioritize them based on importance. Use techniques like the Pomodoro Technique—working in focused intervals followed by short breaks—**to maintain concentration.**

Example:

Sarah, a busy professional, applies the Pomodoro Technique to manage her workload effectively. She sets a timer for 25 minutes and focuses solely on a specific task, such as drafting an email or reviewing a report. During the break intervals, she steps away from her desk to stretch and refresh her mind. This structured approach helps Sarah stay focused and productive amidst distractions.

Digital Detox: Set boundaries with technology by scheduling "unplugged" periods during the day. Turn off non-essential notifications and create designated times to check emails and social media.

Example:

John implements a digital detox routine during evenings to unwind and foster mental clarity. He sets a time limit for screen use, engages in offline activities like reading or meditating, and prioritizes quality time with loved ones. By disconnecting from digital distractions, John creates space for introspection and relaxation.

Single-Tasking: Ever feel like you're doing a million things at once but getting very little result? That's the life of a multitasker. Single tasking, on the other hand, is about giving your full attention to one task at a time. Let's break down the differences with practical examples:

Example:

Emily, a student preparing for exams, practices single-tasking to optimize her study sessions. Instead of trying to study while scrolling through social media, she dedicates uninterrupted blocks of time to each subject. By focusing solely on the task at hand, Emily absorbs information more effectively and retains knowledge for exams.

During a busy day at home, you decide to declutter your living space. Instead of trying to multitask by responding to emails and messages while tidying up, you commit to single-tasking. As you focus solely on organizing one area at a time, you notice a sense of calm and clarity emerging.

Mindful Breathing: Use mindful breathing exercises to anchor your attention and calm a busy mind. Practice deep, intentional breaths to center yourself and let go of mental chatter.

Example:

Before an important meeting, Alex engages in mindful breathing to cultivate mental clarity and composure. By taking slow, deliberate breaths, Alex reduces anxiety and enhances focus. This simple mindfulness practice prepares Alex to approach the meeting with confidence and presence.

Before an important meeting, you take a few minutes to practice mindful breathing. As you inhale and exhale deeply, you feel a sense of calm wash over you. This brief mindfulness exercise helps clear mental clutter and enhance focus.

Physical Movement: Incorporate movement into your routine to release pent-up energy and improve mental clarity. Activities like yoga, walking, or dancing can be effective in grounding your attention and promoting relaxation.

Example:

After a long day of work, Lisa rejuvenates her mind and body with a brisk walk in nature. As she immerses herself in the sights and sounds of the outdoors, Lisa experiences a sense of clarity and renewed energy. Physical movement serves as a powerful antidote to mental fatigue and enhances overall well-being.

After a long day of work, you unwind with a yoga session. As you move through the poses mindfully, you notice tensions melting away, leaving you feeling refreshed and mentally clear.

How to avoid distractions and stay focused

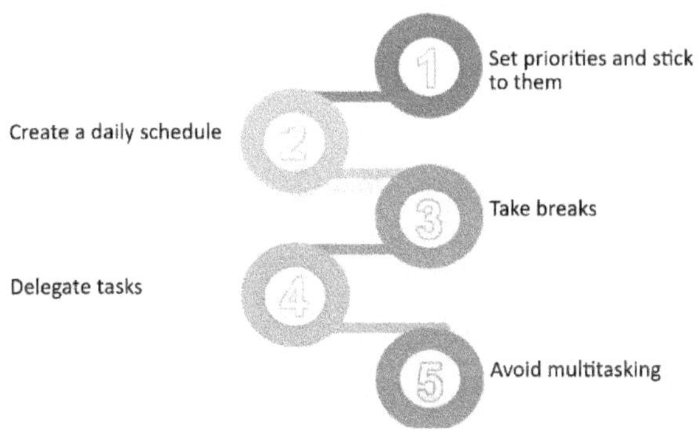

Conclusion

Cultivating mental clarity is an ongoing practice that requires intention and commitment. By letting go of distractions and nurturing focused attention, you can enhance productivity, reduce stress, and experience greater clarity in daily life.

CHAPTER 5

TAMING THE WANDERING MIND: STRATEGIES FOR CONCENTRATION

"Concentration is the cornerstone of productivity. By mastering the art of focus, you transform fleeting moments into powerful acts of creation." - **Abilasha U R**

In previous chapters, you explored the power of mindfulness and self-reflection. Now, we delve into the challenge of concentration – the ability to direct and sustain your attention on a chosen task. In our fast-paced world, filled with distractions and mental clutter, achieving focused concentration can feel like trying to hold onto smoke. But fear not! This chapter equips you with practical strategies to tame your wandering mind and cultivate laser-sharp focus.

Why Concentration Matters?

Focus your mind, fuel your creation!

Strong concentration is the cornerstone of productivity and achievement. It allows you to:

Deepen Learning: When you focus intently on the material you're studying, you retain information more effectively and develop a deeper understanding.

Imagine you're studying for a biology exam. With focused concentration, you can delve into complex concepts like cellular respiration, truly understanding the intricate dance of molecules within a cell. You're not just passively memorizing facts; you're actively engaging with the material, forming strong neural connections that solidify your understanding. This focused attention allows you to retain information more effectively for tests and future application.

Let's take another Scenario, Mark, a college student, struggles to concentrate while studying for his history exam. He constantly checks his phone, gets sidetracked by social media notifications, and finds himself daydreaming about upcoming weekend plans. As a result, he has difficulty grasping key historical events and struggles to recall important details when taking the exam.

Enhance Work Performance: Focused attention allows you to complete tasks with greater accuracy and efficiency, leading to improved work quality and productivity.

Let's say you're a graphic designer working on a crucial client presentation. With focused concentration, you can meticulously craft a design that resonates with the target audience. You're not making careless mistakes or overlooking crucial details. Your focused attention allows you to complete the project efficiently and with high quality, impressing your client and boosting your professional reputation.

*Let's consider Sarah, a marketing professional, often struggles to focus at work. While writing a report, she gets pulled into email threads unrelated to the task, checks social media updates, and constantly feels the urge to multitask. This fragmented attention leads to errors in her report, missed deadlines, and frustration from both her and her colleagues.***Boost Creativity:** When your mind is free from distractions, it can enter a state of flow, where creativity flourishes and innovative ideas emerge.

Imagine you're a musician composing a new song. With focused concentration, you can tap into your creative wellspring, letting the melody and lyrics flow freely. You're not inhibited by self-doubt or distractions. Your focused mind allows you to experiment with different sounds and ideas, leading to a truly original and captivating piece of music.

David, a writer, finds his creativity stifled by a wandering mind. While working on a novel, he constantly gets sidetracked by research rabbit holes, perfectionist tendencies, and comparing himself to other authors. His inability to focus hinders his creative flow, making it difficult to develop a compelling storyline and characters.

Increase Well-being: Improved concentration reduces stress, anxiety, and feelings of overwhelm, promoting a sense of calm and mental clarity.

Constant distractions and a wandering mind can be mentally draining. Imagine finally settling down with a good book after a long day. With focused concentration, you can immerse yourself in the story, escaping from daily worries and anxieties. Your mind quiets down, and you experience a sense of calm and mental clarity. Improved concentration reduces stress and allows you to recharge your mental batteries, fostering greater well-being.

After a hectic day at work, Maria tries to unwind by reading a novel. However, she finds herself constantly checking her phone, replaying conversations in her head, and worrying about upcoming deadlines. This fragmented attention prevents her from truly enjoying the book, leaving her feeling stressed and mentally fatigued.

Understanding the Wandering Mind

Our minds are naturally wired to be curious and flit from one thought to another. This constant mental chatter, however, can disrupt concentration and hinder our ability to focus on the task at hand. Here are some common culprits behind a wandering mind:

Distractions: From buzzing notifications to social media feeds, external distractions constantly vie for our attention.**Internal Distractions:** Worries, anxieties, and even daydreams can hijack our focus and pull our attention away from the present moment.**Lack of Motivation**: When we find a task uninteresting or challenging, our minds are more likely to wander in search of something more stimulating.

Strategies for Taming Your Wandering Mind

Our minds are like curious butterflies, flitting from one flower to the next, easily captivated by fleeting stimuli. The good news is that you can train your mind to be more focused. Here are some practical strategies you can incorporate into your daily life:

1. Mindfulness Meditation:

Think of your mind as a muscle that needs training. Mindfulness meditation is like going to the gym for your focus. By observing your thoughts and emotions without judgment, you become aware of distractions arising in your mind. This awareness empowers you to gently redirect your attention back to the present moment and the task at hand.

Imagine Sarah, a busy entrepreneur, constantly overwhelmed by a to-do list that seems to grow longer by the minute. She struggles to focus on any one task for long, as her mind jumps from one project to another. Sarah incorporates mindfulness meditation into her daily routine. By taking 10 minutes each morning to focus on her breath and observe her thoughts without judgment, she strengthens her ability to concentrate and prioritize tasks effectively.

2. The Power of Setting Intentions:

Before diving headfirst into a task, take a moment to set a clear intention. What do you want to achieve? Is it completing a specific section of a report, finishing a chapter in your novel, or tackling a challenging math problem? Setting a clear intention helps your mind prioritize the task at hand and reduces the allure of distractions.

David, a software developer, often finds himself getting sidetracked while coding. He starts working on a new feature but gets lured into checking emails, fixing minor bugs in unrelated areas, and responding to online messages. David starts setting clear intentions before starting his coding sessions. He might say to himself, "My intention for the next hour is to finish implementing this specific user interface function." This clear focus allows him to stay on track and avoid distractions.

3. The Pomodoro Technique:

This popular time management strategy is a game-changer for focus. Break down your work into focused intervals, typically 25 minutes, followed by short breaks. Set a timer and work intently on a single task until the timer goes off. Then, reward yourself with a short break (5 minutes) to refresh your mind before returning to the task. The Pomodoro Technique helps maintain focus and prevents burnout from staring at a screen for extended periods.

Maria, a writer, struggles to maintain focus while working on her novel. She often gets bogged down by writer's block and finds herself checking social media mindlessly. Maria starts using the Pomodoro Technique. She sets a timer for 25 minutes, commits to writing continuously during that interval, and then allows herself a quick break to stretch or grab a drink. This structured approach helps her stay focused on writing and make consistent progress on her novel.

4. Creating a Focused Environment:

Your workspace has a profound impact on your ability to concentrate. Imagine trying to write a complex legal document in a cluttered, noisy coffee shop. Not ideal, right? To tame your wandering mind, create a focused environment that minimizes distractions. Silence notifications on your phone and computer, turn off unnecessary apps, and declutter your desk. If possible, find a quiet space to work where you won't be interrupted.

Mark, a student, often struggles to concentrate while studying in his dorm room. His roommates play video games, his phone constantly buzzes with notifications, and his desk is overflowing with papers and clutter. Mark decides to create a dedicated study space in the library. He finds a quiet corner, puts his phone on silent mode, and uses noise-canceling headphones. This focused environment allows him to concentrate on his studies and retain information more effectively.

5. Schedule Time for Distractions:

Let's face it, sometimes the urge to check social media or browse the internet becomes overwhelming. Instead of constantly battling this urge, schedule specific times for these activities. This allows you to focus on the task at hand without guilt and indulge in distractions during designated breaks.

Sarah, a marketing professional, finds herself mindlessly scrolling through social media throughout the workday. This constant distraction hinders her productivity and increases stress levels. Sarah implements a "distraction detox" strategy. She schedules specific times during her lunch break and after work to check social media and personal emails. During work hours, she keeps her phone on silent and avoids social media platforms, allowing her to focus on her work tasks without interruption.

6. Prioritize Sleep: When you're well-rested, your concentration and focus naturally improve. Aim for 7-8 hours of quality sleep each night.

Just like your phone needs to recharge to function optimally, so does your brain. When you're sleep-deprived, your attention span dwindles, and your mind struggles to stay focused. You become more susceptible to distractions and find it challenging to retain information.

Imagine Lily, a college student constantly battling late-night study sessions and early morning classes. Sleep deprivation makes it difficult for her to concentrate during lectures. Information feels blurry, and she finds herself daydreaming or doodling instead of taking notes. Lily prioritizes getting a good night's sleep by establishing a regular sleep schedule, creating a relaxing bedtime routine, and avoiding screens before bed. With sufficient sleep, Lily notices a significant improvement in her focus and concentration during lectures. She can absorb information more effectively and retain key concepts for exams.

7. Engage in Physical Activity: Regular exercise not only improves physical health but also enhances cognitive function and concentration.

Physical activity isn't just about building muscle and burning calories. It also has a profound impact on your brain. Exercise increases blood flow to the brain, promoting the growth of new brain cells and improving the connections between them. This translates to enhanced cognitive function, sharper focus, and improved concentration.

David, a programmer, often feels sluggish and mentally foggy throughout his workday. Sitting for extended periods at his desk takes a toll on his concentration and productivity. David incorporates regular exercise into his routine by taking brisk walks during lunch breaks or attending a gym class after work. The physical activity not only improves his physical health but also boosts his cognitive function. David finds himself focusing more easily on complex coding tasks and experiencing a general sense of mental clarity throughout the day.

Remember: Cultivating concentration is a journey, not a destination. There will be days when your mind wanders. The key is to acknowledge these distractions without judgment, gently refocus your attention, and persevere with practice. Over time, you'll develop the mental discipline to tame your wandering mind and achieve a state of focused concentration that empowers you to excel in all areas of your life.

Bonus Tip: Consider incorporating brain training exercises or games designed to improve focus and attention. These exercises can be a fun and engaging way to strengthen your concentration skills.

CHAPTER 6

THE PRACTICE OF NON-JUDGMENT: ACCEPTANCE IN THE PRESENT MOMENT

"Peace arrives with open arms, not judgment."
– Abilasha U R

Have you ever felt like your inner critic is constantly on blast? You're trying to enjoy a moment, but a voice whispers judgments about your appearance, your actions, or even the weather. This internal chatter can be relentless, pulling us away from the present moment and causing unnecessary stress.

Our mind just like a judging machine, whatever we experience in daily life it will get categorized and filtered to good, bad and neutral. It's the nature of the mind to judge.

YOUR MIND JUDGES EVERY EXPERIENCE

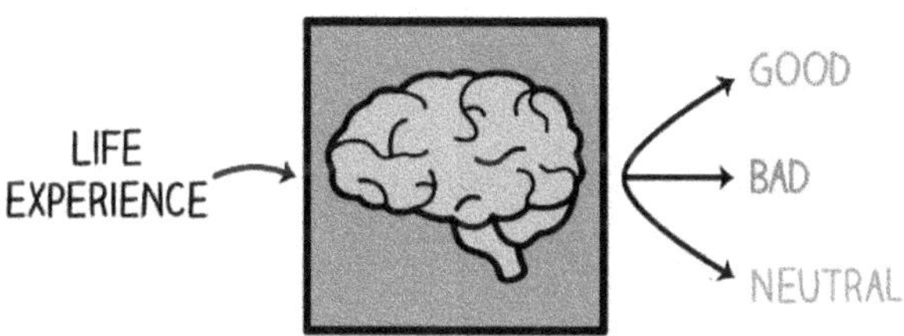

But what if there was a way to quiet that voice and simply experience life as it is? This is where the practice of non-judgment comes in. Non-judgment isn't about shutting down your thoughts and feelings. It's about observing them without labeling them as good or bad. It's like watching clouds drift by in the sky – you acknowledge them, but you don't judge their shape or how fast they're moving. This chapter introduces the concept of non-judgment and its powerful role in cultivating inner peace and mental well-being.

Sometimes, these judgments are helpful. They can lead you to understand the things that bring you up, give you energy, and fill you with purpose. They can help you understand what doesn't resonate with you, and leaves you feeling drained.

But when left unchecked, the judging mind is taxing and controlling. It takes significant energy to evaluate every experience you encounter. There's always something to be done about wherever you are.

Chase the "good"

Flee from the "bad"

And ignore the "neutral"

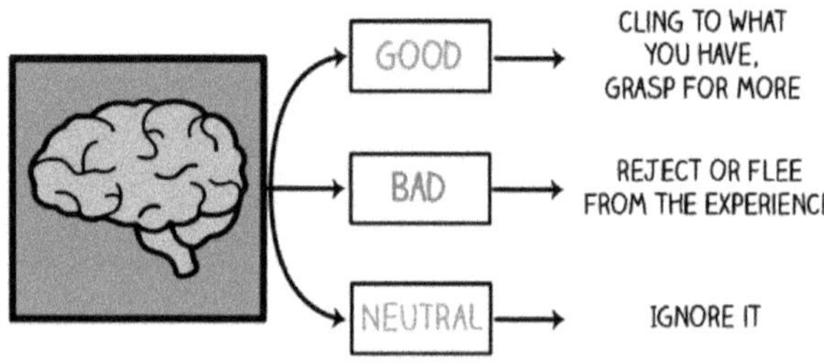

Why Non-Judgment Matters

Imagine yourself stuck in a traffic jam. Your mind races with judgments: "This is ridiculous! Why is everyone such a bad driver?" Frustration and anger build, adding to your stress and making the situation even more unpleasant.

Now, consider a different approach. Practicing non-judgment allows you to accept the traffic jam as it is, a temporary inconvenience. You can acknowledge your frustration without judgment, perhaps focusing on calming your breath or listening to calming music. This acceptance fosters a sense of inner peace, even amidst external chaos.

Why is Non-Judgment Important?

Constant judgment is a major source of negativity in our lives. It fuels stress, anxiety, and keeps us dwelling on the past or worrying about the future. When we practice non-judgment, we allow ourselves to be fully present in the current moment. We can appreciate the good things without inflating them with expectations, and we can acknowledge the difficult things without getting swept away by negativity. This can lead to a more peaceful mind, increased self-compassion, and even better relationships with others.

non-judgment, means letting go of the automatic judgments that arise in your mind with every experience you have.

Setting down the judging mind, even for a short while, is a refreshing weight off of your shoulders.

In practicing non-judgment, there's no longer anything to be done about the present moment. No grasping for more, no resisting what's there, and no ignoring of life's experience.

When you stop trying to react to your experience, you can open up to it completely, resting in mindful presence.

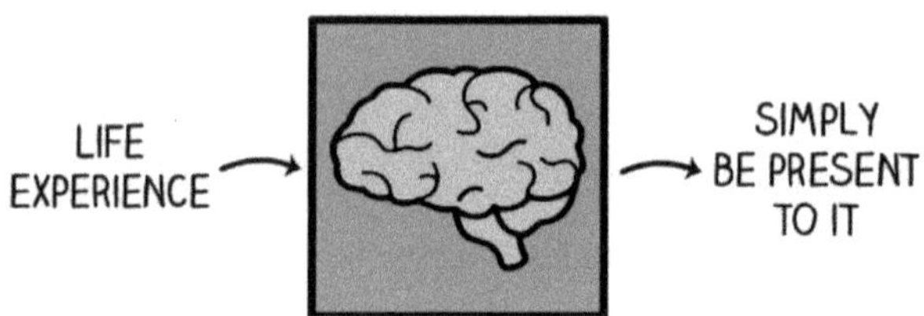

Here are some key benefits of embracing non-judgment:

Reduced Stress and Anxiety: When we constantly judge ourselves and our situations, stress and anxiety levels rise. Non-judgment allows us to let go of negativity and cultivate a calmer, more accepting state of mind.

Improved Relationships: Judgmental thoughts about others can create distance and conflict in our relationships. By practicing non-judgment, we can approach others with an open mind and greater compassion.

Enhanced Self-Esteem: Our inner critic can be relentless, chipping away at our self-worth. Non-judgment allows us to observe our thoughts and feelings without judgment, fostering self-acceptance and a more positive self-image.

Greater Mindfulness: Non-judgment is a cornerstone of mindfulness practice. By observing our thoughts and feelings without judgment, we become more aware of the present moment and less caught up in the mental chatter.

Non-Judgment in Everyday Life

Non-judgment isn't about suppressing emotions or pretending everything is perfect. It's about acknowledging your thoughts and feelings without attaching a positive or negative label. Here are some practical tips to incorporate non-judgment into your daily life:

1. Notice Your Judgments:

The first step is becoming aware of your internal judgments. Pay attention to your self-talk and how you perceive situations. Are you constantly criticizing yourself or others?

a writer, constantly judges her work as "not good enough" or compares herself to other successful authors. This self-judgment leads to feelings of inadequacy and hinders her creativity.

2. Label Your Thoughts:

Once you notice a judgment, simply label it as a "thought" or "judgment." This act of acknowledging the thought without attaching to it creates space for observation.

During a yoga class, Mark finds himself judging his flexibility compared to others. He recognizes this as a judgmental thought and labels it internally, "This is a judgment about my flexibility."

3. Breathe and Observe:

Take a few deep breaths and observe your judgment without judgment. Where does it come from? What emotions are attached to it?

While giving a presentation, Maria feels a wave of anxiety and judges herself for being nervous. She takes a deep breath and observes the feeling of anxiety without judgment. She realizes the feeling is normal and doesn't define her ability to deliver the presentation.

4. Accept and Let Go:

Finally, accept the judgment as simply a thought and gently let it go. Focus your attention on the present moment and the task at hand.

During a heated discussion, David feels the urge to judge the other person's viewpoint. He acknowledges this urge, takes a deep breath, and chooses to listen with open-mindedness instead of judgment.

Remember: Non-judgment is a powerful tool for cultivating inner peace and living a more fulfilling life. By observing our thoughts and feelings without judgment, we can become more present, compassionate, and resilient. Start small with these practices, and you'll be surprised by how much more you can appreciate the beauty of the present moment. Remember, acceptance is not resignation – it's the first step towards positive change. As Jack Kornfield says, **"*You are worthy of acceptance, exactly as you are.*"** Embrace the present moment, imperfections, and all.

Bonus Tip: Consider incorporating mindfulness meditation into your daily routine. Meditation helps cultivate a sense of present moment awareness and allows you to observe your thoughts and feelings without judgment.

By embracing non-judgment, you create space for greater peace, acceptance, and connection in your life. Remember, "Mind Your Own Mind" and cultivate a kinder, more accepting inner dialogue for a more fulfilling and joyful experience of life.

CHAPTER 7

EMBRACING IMPERMANENCE: FINDING PEACE IN CHANGE

Change is life's rhythm. Flow with it, find peace
– Abilasha U R

Life is an ever-flowing river, constantly shifting and changing. Clinging to the illusion of permanence can lead to suffering and disappointment. This chapter explores the concept of impermanence and how embracing change, both big and small, can lead to a more peaceful and fulfilling life.

Understanding Impermanence

Everything in life is impermanent and imperfections. Relationships change, jobs come and go, seasons turn, and even our own bodies are constantly in flux. Yet, we often resist this reality, clinging to the past or fearing the uncertainties of the future. This resistance creates inner conflict and hinders our ability to adapt and thrive in a changing world.

The Challenges of Impermanence

Loss and Grief: When faced with loss, whether a loved one, a job, or a cherished possession, we experience grief. Accepting the impermanence of life helps us navigate these losses with greater acceptance and move forward.

Scenario: Sarah loses her job due to company downsizing. Initially, she feels devastated and fears the financial instability. By gradually accepting the situation and recognizing it as a part of life's ebb and flow, she starts focusing on her skills and passions. Sarah decides to pursue freelance work in her field, eventually finding more satisfaction and flexibility than she had in her previous job.

Fear of the Unknown: The future is uncertain, and this uncertainty can be frightening. Embracing impermanence allows us to let go of the need for control and embrace the possibilities that change can bring.

Scenario: Raj, an entrepreneur, is anxious about the future of his startup amidst economic uncertainties. Instead of letting fear paralyze him, he adopts a flexible mindset, constantly adapting his business strategies to new market trends. This approach not only helps his business survive but also thrive in a volatile market.

Dissatisfaction with the Present: If we constantly yearn for the past or worry about the future, we miss the beauty and richness of the present moment. Accepting impermanence helps us appreciate the here and now.

Scenario: Emily is always nostalgic about her college days and anxious about her future. This prevents her from enjoying her current job and social life. By practicing mindfulness and embracing the impermanence of life, she starts to appreciate her present moments, finding joy in her current experiences and relationships.

Finding Peace in Change

While impermanence can be challenging, it also presents opportunities for growth and transformation. Here are some ways to cultivate peace with change:

Mindfulness Practice: Mindfulness helps anchor you in the present moment, allowing you to accept whatever arises without judgment.

Focus on What You Can Control: Focus your energy on the things you can control, such as your thoughts, actions, and reactions to change.

Develop a Growth Mindset: View challenges as opportunities for learning and growth. Embrace change as a chance to develop new skills and experiences.

Practice Letting Go: Learn to let go of the past and attachments that hold you back. Focus on what is happening now and what you can create in the present moment.

Scenario: David, a recent college graduate, feels lost and unsure about his future career path. He's afraid of making the "wrong" decision and getting stuck in a job he doesn't enjoy. By embracing impermanence, David realizes that his career path doesn't have to be set in stone. He can explore different options, learn new skills, and adjust his course as he goes. This acceptance of change empowers him to approach his job search with a more open and flexible mind.

Impermanence and Happiness

Embracing impermanence doesn't mean giving up on your dreams or goals. It simply means accepting that life is a journey, full of unexpected twists and turns. By acknowledging this reality, you can find peace with change and cultivate a sense of happiness that isn't dependent on external circumstances.

Living with a Beginner's Mind:

Approach life with a beginner's mind, open to new experiences and possibilities. Embrace the impermanence of each moment and find joy in the ever-changing flow of life.

Now let me decide to take up painting as a hobby. With no prior experience, i approaches each painting session with a beginner's mind, enjoying the process of creation without any expectations. This mindset helps me find joy and relaxation in the activity, regardless of the outcome.

Remember: Change is inevitable. By learning to embrace impermanence, you can unlock a greater sense of peace, resilience, and adaptability in the face of life's inevitable transitions.

CHAPTER 8

GRATITUDE AND PRESENCE: FOSTERING APPRECIATION FOR THE NOW

Gratitude and mindfulness ground us in the present, revealing the beauty in each moment.
– Abilasha U R

Life can often feel like a whirlwind of tasks, deadlines, and responsibilities. We rush from one thing to the next, **rarely taking the time to appreciate the beauty and wonder of the present moment.** This chapter explores the powerful practices of gratitude and mindfulness, offering tools to cultivate a sense of contentment and savor the richness of everyday life.

The Power of Gratitude

Gratitude is more than simply saying "**THANK YOU.**" It's a conscious attitude of *appreciation for the positive aspects of life, both big and* small. Research shows that cultivating gratitude has a profound impact on our well-being, leading to:

Increased Happiness: By focusing on the good things in our lives, we shift our perspective away from negativity and towards a more positive outlook.

Enhanced Relationships: Expressing gratitude to others strengthens our bonds and fosters feelings of connection and appreciation.

Improved Resilience: Gratitude helps us weather life's challenges by reminding us of the things we have to be thankful for, even during difficult times.

Greater Well-Being: Studies show that practicing gratitude can lead to improved sleep, reduced stress, and a stronger immune system.

Practicing Gratitude in Everyday Life

Robert Emmons, psychology professor and gratitude researcher at the University of California, Davis, explains that there are two key components of practicing gratitude:

1. We affirm the good things we've received

2. We acknowledge the role other people play in providing our lives with goodness

Most of us know it's important to express thanks to the people who help us, or silently acknowledge the things we are grateful for in life. Research has linked gratitude with a wide range of benefits, including strengthening your immune system and improving sleep patterns, feeling optimistic and experiencing more joy and pleasure, being more helpful and generous, and feeling less lonely and isolated.

10 Ways to Practice Daily Gratitude

As Jon Kabat-Zinn says, "The little things? The little moments? They aren't little." Saying thank you, holding the door for someone, these little moments can change the tone of your whole day.

One of the most powerful ways to rewire your brain for more joy and less stress is to focus on gratitude. Here are 10 simple ways to become more grateful:

1. Keep a Gratitude Journal: Establish a daily practice in which you remind yourself of the gifts, grace, benefits, and good things you enjoy. Recalling moments of gratitude associated with ordinary events, your personal attributes, or valued people in your life gives you the potential to interweave a sustainable theme of gratefulness into your life.

2. Remember the Bad : To be grateful in your current state, it is helpful to remember the hard times that you once experienced. When you remember how difficult life used to be and how far you have come, you set up an explicit contrast in your mind, and this contrast is fertile ground for gratefulness.

3. Ask Yourself Three Questions: Meditate on your relationships with parents, friends, siblings, work associates, children, and partners using these three questions: "What have I received from __?", "What have I given to __?", and "What troubles and difficulty have I caused?"

4. Share Your Gratitude with Others: Research has found that expressing gratitude can strengthen relationships. So the next time your partner, friend or family member does something you appreciate, be sure to let them know.

5. Come to Your Senses: Through our senses—the ability to touch, see, smell, taste, and hear—we gain an appreciation of what it means to be human and of what an incredible miracle it is to be alive. Seen through the lens of gratitude, the human body is not only a miraculous construction, but also a gift.

6. Use Visual Reminders: Because the two primary obstacles to gratefulness are forgetfulness and a lack of mindful awareness, visual reminders can serve as cues to trigger thoughts of gratitude. Often times, the best visual reminders are other people.

7. Make a Vow to Practice Gratitude: Research shows that making an oath to perform a behavior increases the likelihood that the action will be executed. Therefore, write your own gratitude vow, which could be as simple as "I vow to count my blessings each day," and post it somewhere where you will be reminded of it every day.

8. Watch Your Language: Grateful people have a particular linguistic style that uses the language of gifts, givers, blessings, blessed, fortune, fortunate, and abundance. In gratitude, you should not focus on how inherently good you are, but rather on the inherently good things that others have done on your behalf.

9. Go Through the Motions: Grateful motions include smiling, saying thank you, and writing letters of gratitude. By "going through grateful motions," you'll trigger the emotion of gratitude more often.

10. Think Outside the Box: If you want to make the most out of opportunities to flex your gratitude muscles, you must look creatively for new situations and circumstances in which to feel grateful. Please write the creative ways you've found to help you practice gratitude.

Interested in reaping some of these benefits? Get started with a gratitude practice.

Here are some practical ways to incorporate gratitude into your daily routine:

Start a Gratitude Journal: Dedicate a few minutes each day to write down things you're grateful for. This could be anything from a supportive friend to a delicious cup of coffee.

The Gratitude Jar: Fill a jar with small pieces of paper where you write down things you're grateful for. Take a moment each day to pick a piece and reflect on your blessings.

The Gratitude Walk: Take a walk in nature and actively focus on the beauty around you. Appreciate the warmth of the sun, the sound of birds chirping, or the vibrant colors of flowers.

Express Gratitude to Others: Let the people in your life know how much you appreciate them. Write a thank-you note, send a heartfelt text, or simply express your gratitude verbally.

The Art of Mindfulness

Mindfulness is the practice of paying attention to the present moment without judgment. It's about being fully present in your experiences, whether it's savoring a delicious meal, feeling the gentle breeze on your skin, or simply observing your thoughts and emotions without getting caught up in them.

Just like any skill, mindfulness takes practice. Here are some ways to cultivate a more mindful presence:

Mindful Breathing: Take a few minutes each day to focus on your breath. Notice the sensation of your chest rising and falling with each inhalation and exhalation. This simple practice can anchor you in the present moment.

Mindful Eating: Slow down during meals and truly savor your food. Pay attention to the taste, texture, and aroma of each bite.

Mindful Body Scans: Lie down comfortably and focus your attention on different parts of your body. Notice any physical sensations without judgment.

Mindful Activities: Engage in activities that allow you to be fully present, such as gardening, mindful walking, or listening to music with full attention.

Gratitude and Presence: A Powerful Combination

Gratitude and mindfulness work hand-in-hand. By cultivating an attitude of appreciation, we become more aware of the beauty and richness of the present moment. Mindfulness, in turn, allows us to savor these moments with greater depth and appreciation.

Scenario: Imagine Sarah, a busy professional who often feels overwhelmed and stressed. She starts practicing gratitude by writing down three things she's grateful for each morning. She also incorporates mindful walks into her routine, focusing on the sights, sounds, and smells of her surroundings. As Sarah cultivates gratitude and mindfulness, she experiences a shift in her perspective. She starts noticing the good things in her life, appreciates the simple joys of each day, and feels a greater sense of calm and well-being.

Remember: Gratitude and presence are not about achieving a perfect state of mind. It's a continuous journey of cultivating appreciation and awareness in your daily life. By incorporating these practices, you can unlock a greater sense of happiness, peace, and connection to the present moment.

CHAPTER 9

MINDFUL COMMUNICATION: ENGAGING FULLY IN INTERACTIONS

"Listen with intent, speak with authenticity;
mindful communication becomes the bridge to
deeper understanding and richer relationships."
– Abilasha U R

I n our fast-paced world, communication often feels rushed and superficial. We multitask during conversations, formulate responses before the other person finishes speaking, and miss out on the true essence of connection. This chapter explores the power of mindful communication, a practice that fosters deeper understanding, stronger relationships, and more effective interactions.

Why Mindful Communication Matters

Communication is more than just exchanging words. It's about connecting with others on a deeper level, understanding their perspectives, and building meaningful relationships. Here's how mindful communication can enhance your interactions with two different personal and professional scenarios for better understanding each:

Improved Listening: Mindful communication emphasizes active listening, where you truly pay attention to the speaker's words and nonverbal cues. You put aside distractions, ask clarifying questions, and seek to understand the speaker's full message.

Example 1: During a team meeting at work, instead of checking your phone or thinking about your next task, you focus entirely on your colleague's presentation. You notice their enthusiasm through their tone and gestures, and you ask follow-up questions to clarify points you're unsure about. This demonstrates your engagement and helps you fully understand their ideas.

Example 2: When your partner is sharing a concern, you listen without interrupting. You nod and maintain eye contact, showing that you are fully present. After they finish, you summarize what you heard to confirm your understanding: "It sounds like you're feeling overwhelmed with your workload, is that right?"

Enhanced Empathy: By actively listening, you build empathy and understanding. You can see things from the other person's perspective and connect with their emotions on a deeper level.

Example 1: A friend is going through a tough time, and instead of offering immediate advice or comparing their situation to your own, you say, "That sounds really difficult. How are you holding up?" This approach validates their feelings and shows that you are trying to understand their experience from their perspective.

Example 2: A coworker expresses frustration about a project. Instead of dismissing their feelings or getting defensive, you say, "I can see this project has been really challenging for you. Let's figure out how we can make it more manageable." This helps build a supportive environment and fosters mutual understanding.

Reduced Conflict: Misunderstandings often arise from unclear communication. Mindful communication fosters clarity and reduces the potential for conflict.

Example 1: In a disagreement with a family member, you focus on using "I" statements rather than "you" statements. For example, "I feel upset when the dishes are left in the sink because it makes the kitchen feel cluttered," instead of "You never clean up after yourself." This reduces blame and encourages constructive dialogue.

Example 2: During a heated discussion at work, you practice active listening by repeating back the other person's points: "If I understand correctly, you're concerned about the deadline because it impacts our project quality. Is that right?" This approach helps to clarify misunderstandings and reduce potential conflicts.

Stronger Relationships: When you truly connect with others through mindful communication, you build stronger and more meaningful relationships.

Example 1: You make it a habit to have regular, distraction-free conversations with your partner, where you both share your thoughts and feelings openly. This practice strengthens your emotional connection and understanding of each other.

Example 2: At social gatherings, you engage in meaningful conversations by asking open-ended questions like, "What has been the highlight of your week?" rather than superficial ones. This shows genuine interest and helps you form deeper connections with others.

The Art of Mindful Communication

Some practical tips to cultivate mindful communication in our daily interactions:

Be Present: Put away distractions (phones, laptops) and give the speaker your full attention. Make eye contact and show genuine interest in what they have to say.

Listen Actively: Focus on understanding the speaker's message, both verbal and nonverbal. Pay attention to their body language, tone of voice, and underlying emotions.

Ask Clarifying Questions: Don't be afraid to ask questions to ensure you understand the speaker's perspective.

Respond Mindfully: Before responding, take a moment to gather your thoughts and choose your words carefully. Consider the other person's feelings and express yourself clearly and respectfully.

Communicate with Authenticity: Be genuine and express yourself authentically. Let your personality shine through in your communication.

Mindful Communication in Different Scenarios

Difficult Conversations: Mindful communication is especially important during challenging conversations. By remaining calm, actively listening, and focusing on solutions, you can navigate disagreements more effectively.

Nonverbal Communication: Mindful communication goes beyond words. Pay attention to your body language, facial expressions, and tone of voice. Ensure these nonverbal cues are congruent with your spoken words.

The Benefits of Mindful Communication

Several studies have highlighted the positive effects of mindful communication on mental well-being. For example, research has shown that mindful communication reduces stress levels, improves relationship satisfaction, and enhances emotional regulation. Additionally, studies have linked mindfulness practices to reduced symptoms of anxiety and depression, increased self-compassion, and improved overall mental health.

Mindful communication isn't just about improving your interactions with others. It also benefits you in profound ways:

Increased Self-Awareness: By focusing on the present moment and actively listening, you gain a deeper understanding of yourself, your thoughts, and your emotions.

After a stressful day, you take a few moments to reflect on your conversations. You notice that you were more impatient than usual. Recognizing this, you decide to practice deep breathing before your next interaction to stay calm and present.

Reduced Stress: Clear and respectful communication can significantly reduce stress and conflict in your life.

By addressing misunderstandings immediately with clear and respectful communication, you avoid prolonged conflicts and the stress they cause. For instance, if a friend misinterprets your actions, you clarify your intentions promptly, preventing any lingering tension.

Enhanced Well-being: Stronger relationships and a sense of connection contribute to greater overall well-being.

Engaging in mindful communication regularly, you notice that your relationships are becoming more fulfilling. The sense of connection and understanding you gain from these interactions contributes to your overall happiness and mental health.

Remember: Mindful communication is a skill that takes practice. Be patient with yourself, and strive to incorporate these principles into your daily interactions. As you cultivate mindful communication, you'll experience richer connections, deeper understanding, and a more fulfilling life.

CULTIVATING COMPASSION: CONNECTING WITH OTHERS AND OURSELVES

"Compassion guides us to understand and support others with care and empathy through life's challenges." – **Abilasha U R**

Life can be challenging, filled with struggles and setbacks. Compassion, the ability to understand and share the suffering of others (and ourselves), acts as a powerful antidote to hardship. This chapter explores the nature of compassion, its benefits, and practical ways to cultivate it in your daily life.

Understanding Compassion

Compassion is simply a kind, friendly presence in the face of what's difficult. Its power is connecting us with what's difficult—it offers us an approach that differs from the turning away that we usually do.

Compassion goes beyond mere sympathy, which is simply feeling sorry for someone. Compassion involves:

Understanding: Seeking to understand the other person's perspective and the source of their suffering.

Empathy: Feeling what the other person is feeling, putting yourself in their shoes and experiencing their emotions on a deeper level.

Action: A desire to alleviate suffering and offer support, whether through words, actions, or simply a kind presence.

The Importance of Self-Compassion

Compassion isn't just about caring for others. It's equally important to cultivate self-compassion. This means treating yourself with kindness and understanding, especially during difficult times. When we are self-critical and harsh towards ourselves, it hinders our ability to extend compassion to others.

Individuals who are more self-compassionate tend to have greater happiness, life satisfaction and motivation, better relationships and physical health, and less anxiety and depression. They also have the resilience needed to cope with stressful life events such as divorce, health crises, academic failure, and even combat trauma.

When we are mindful of our struggles, and respond to ourselves with compassion, kindness, and support in times of difficulty, things start to change. We can learn to embrace ourselves and our lives, despite inner and outer imperfections, and provide ourselves with the strength needed to thrive.

Repeat these phrases to yourself (or some variation of words that work for you):

- **May I be kind to myself in this moment.**

This breaks the automaticity of our survival responses and negative thought loops.

- **May I accept this moment exactly as it is.**

From William James, considered the founder of American psychology: "Be willing to have it so. Acceptance of what has happened is the first step to overcoming the consequence of any misfortune."

- **May I accept myself exactly as I am in this moment.**

From humanist psychologist Carl Rogers: "The curious paradox is that when I accept myself exactly as I am, then I can change."

- **May I give myself all the compassion I need.**

Compassion is a resource for resilience, and you are as deserving of your own compassion as others are.

Continue repeating the phrases until you can feel the internal shift: The compassion and kindness and care for yourself becoming stronger than the original negative emotion.

Pause and reflect on your experience. Notice if any possibilities of wise action arise.

Self-compassion depends on honest, direct contact with our own vulnerability. Compassion fully blossoms when we actively offer care to ourselves. To help people address feelings of insecurity and unworthiness, I often introduce mindfulness and compassion through a meditation I call the **RAIN** of Self-Compassion. The acronym RAIN, first coined about 20 years ago by Michele McDonald, is an easy-to-remember tool for practicing mindfulness. It has four steps:

1. Recognize what is going on

2. Allow the experience to be there, just as it is

3. Investigate with kindness

4. Natural awareness, which comes from not identifying with the experience

You can take your time and explore RAIN as a stand-alone meditation or move through the steps in a more abbreviated way whenever challenging feelings arise.

R—Recognize What's Going On

Recognizing means consciously acknowledging, in any given moment, the thoughts, feelings, and behaviors that are affecting us. Like awakening from a dream, the first step out of the trance of unworthiness is simply to recognize that we are stuck, subject to painfully constructing beliefs, emotions, and physical sensations. Common signs of the trance include a critical inner voice, feelings of shame or fear, the squeeze of anxiety or the weight of depression in the body.

A—Allowing: Taking a Life-Giving Pause

Allowing means letting the thoughts, emotions, feelings, or sensations we have recognized simply be there. Typically, when we have an unpleasant experience, we react in one of three ways: by piling on the judgment; by numbing ourselves to our feelings; or by focusing our attention elsewhere.

We allow by simply pausing with the intention to relax our resistance and let the experience be just as it is. Allowing our thoughts, emotions, or bodily sensations simply to be doesn't mean we agree with our conviction that we're unworthy.

I—Investigating with Kindness

Investigating means calling on our natural curiosity—the desire to know truth—and directing a more focused attention to our present experience. Simply pausing to ask, what is happening inside me? can initiate recognition, but investigation adds a more active and pointed kind of inquiry. You might ask yourself: What most wants attention? How am I experiencing this in my body? What am I believing? What does this feeling want from me?

N—Natural Loving Awareness

Natural loving awareness occurs when identification with the self is loosened. This practice of non-identification means that our sense of who we are is not fused with any limiting emotions, sensations, or stories.

Though the first three steps of RAIN require some intentional activity, the N is the treasure: A liberating homecoming to our true nature. There's nothing to do for this last part of RAIN; we simply rest in natural awareness.

The RAIN of Self-Compassion is not a one-shot meditation, nor is the realization of our natural awareness necessarily full, stable, or enduring. Rather, as you practice you may experience a sense of warmth and openness, a shift in perspective. You can trust this! RAIN is a practice for life—meeting our doubts and fears with a healing presence. Each time you are willing to slow down and recognize, oh, this is the trance of unworthiness... this is fear... this is hurt...this is judgment..., you are poised to de-condition the old habits and limiting self-beliefs that imprison your heart. Gradually, you'll experience natural loving awareness as the truth of who you are, more than any story you ever told yourself about being "not good enough" or "basically flawed."

We each have the conditioning to live for long stretches of time imprisoned by a sense of deficiency, cut off from realizing our intrinsic intelligence, aliveness, and love. The greatest blessing, we can give ourselves is to recognize the pain of this trance, and regularly offer a cleansing rain of self-compassion to our awakening hearts.

The Benefits of Compassion

Cultivating compassion has numerous benefits for both us and those around us:

Reduced Stress and Anxiety: Compassion allows us to view challenges with greater perspective and fosters a sense of inner peace.

Stronger Relationships: Compassion fosters connection and strengthens relationships. Others feel seen, heard, and understood when we approach them with compassion.

Increased Well-being: Research shows that compassion leads to greater happiness, life satisfaction, and overall well-being.

Improved Social Interactions: Compassionate individuals are more likely to build positive and supportive relationships.

Developing Your Compassionate Mind

Here are some ways to cultivate compassion in your daily life:

Mindfulness Practice: Developing mindfulness allows you to become more aware of the suffering of others (and yourself).

Loving-Kindness Meditation: This meditation practice cultivates feelings of kindness and well-being towards yourself and others.

Random Acts of Kindness: Perform small acts of kindness for others, such as holding a door open, offering a compliment, or donating to a worthy cause.

Gratitude Practice: Shifting your focus to the good things in your life fosters a sense of appreciation and opens your heart to the suffering of others.

Acknowledge Your Own Pain: Recognizing and accepting your own struggles allows you to better understand and empathize with the pain of others.

Scenario: Sarah, a social worker, often feels overwhelmed by the suffering of her clients. She starts practicing self-compassion by acknowledging her own emotional needs and taking time for self-care. She also incorporates loving-kindness meditation into her daily routine, sending wishes for well-being to herself and others. By cultivating self-compassion, Sarah finds herself better equipped to offer genuine compassion to her clients, leading to more fulfilling and impactful interactions.

Compassion and Social Change

Compassion is not just a personal quality; it's a driving force for positive social change. By fostering a more compassionate society, we can create a world with less suffering and greater connection.

Remember: Compassion is a journey, not a destination. There will be times when anger, frustration, or judgment arise. The key is to acknowledge these feelings with kindness, refocus on cultivating compassion, and connect with yourself and others in a more meaningful way. By opening your heart to compassion, you can create a ripple effect of kindness and understanding that touches everyone in your life.

CHAPTER 11

INTEGRATING MINDFULNESS INTO DAILY LIFE: PRACTICAL APPLICATIONS

"Embrace mindfulness in your daily life for inner peace and present-moment awareness." - **Abilasha U R**

You've explored the power of mindfulness and its potential to cultivate focus, acceptance, and compassion. Now, it's time to translate theory into practice. This chapter equips you with practical tools and strategies to seamlessly integrate mindfulness into your daily routine, transforming your everyday activities into opportunities for present-moment awareness.

Making Mindfulness a Habit

Mindfulness isn't a one-time event; it's a lifelong practice. The key to reaping its benefits lies in consistent application. Here are some tips to make mindfulness a regular habit:

Start Small: Don't overwhelm yourself by trying to meditate for hours on end. Begin with short mindfulness exercises, like mindful breathing for 5 minutes a day, and gradually increase the duration as you become more comfortable.

Schedule Mindfulness: Treat mindfulness like any other important appointment. Block time in your calendar for meditation, mindful walks, or mindful eating.

Find a Mindfulness Buddy: Partnering with a friend or family member who's also interested in mindfulness can provide encouragement and support. Sharing your experiences can deepen your practice.

Anchor Mindfulness in Daily Activities: Look for opportunities to weave mindfulness into your existing routines. Bring mindful awareness to activities like brushing your teeth, washing dishes, or commuting to work.

Mindfulness Throughout Your Day

Here are specific strategies to integrate mindfulness into various aspects of your daily life:

Morning Mindfulness: Start your day with a short mindfulness meditation or mindful stretches. Set an intention for the day, focusing on what you want to cultivate (calmness, focus, etc.).

Mindful Eating: Slow down during meals. Put away distractions and focus on the experience of eating. Notice the colors, textures, and flavors of your food. Savor each bite without judgment.

Mindful Movement: Exercise becomes a mindfulness practice when you focus on your body's sensations. Notice your breath, the movement of your muscles, and the feeling of your feet hitting the ground during a walk or run.

Mindful Communication: Approach conversations with full attention. Listen actively to the speaker, both verbally and nonverbally. Express yourself clearly and with intention.

Mindful Technology Use: In our tech-driven world, mindful technology use is crucial. Set boundaries around screen time. Schedule technology breaks and be present in the moment when you're not using electronic devices.

Beyond Formal Practices

Mindfulness isn't limited to meditation or specific exercises. It's a way of being present in every moment. Here are some ways to cultivate mindfulness throughout your day:

The "Mindful Pause": Throughout your day, take short "mindful pauses." Close your eyes, take a few deep breaths, and simply observe your thoughts and feelings without judgment.

The "Mindful Moment": Choose a mundane activity (washing dishes, making coffee) and turn it into a mindful moment by focusing on all your senses and the present experience.

The "Gratitude Shower": While showering, take a moment to appreciate the feeling of warm water on your skin, the cleansing lather, or the refreshing scent of your soap. Extend this gratitude to other aspects of your daily life.

Remember: Integrating mindfulness is a journey of exploration. Experiment with different techniques and find what works best for you. There's no right or wrong way to be mindful. The key is to cultivate present-moment awareness and bring a sense of calmness and clarity to your everyday experiences.

Bonus Tip: Consider exploring mindfulness apps or online resources that offer guided meditations, mindful movement exercises, and other tools to support your practice.

By weaving mindfulness into the fabric of your daily life, you'll cultivate a greater sense of peace, focus, and well-being, allowing you to navigate life's challenges with greater resilience and appreciate the beauty and wonder of each moment.

CHAPTER 12

OVERCOMING CHALLENGES ON THE PATH TO PRESENCE

"Yesterday is history, tomorrow is a mystery, today is a gift. That's why it's called the present." **- Elbert Hubbard**

The journey to a more mindful and present life is filled with both rewards and obstacles. This chapter explores some common challenges you might encounter and equips you with strategies to overcome them and stay committed to your practice.

Common Challenges on the Path to Presence

The Wandering Mind: Our minds naturally wander. Don't get discouraged if you find your thoughts drifting during meditation or mindfulness exercises. Acknowledge the wandering mind gently and refocus your attention on the present moment.

Self-Doubt and Judgment: It's natural to question your progress or judge yourself for not being "mindful enough." Remember, mindfulness is a practice, not a destination. Be kind to yourself and celebrate your efforts.

Boredom and Restlessness: Mindfulness can feel uneventful at times. This is an opportunity to train your mind to find peace and contentment in stillness. Observe your boredom without judgment and allow it to pass.

Discomfort with Emotions: Mindfulness can bring up uncomfortable emotions you may have been avoiding. Acknowledge these emotions with compassion and allow yourself to feel them without judgment.

Lack of Time: Everyone feels busy. The key is to integrate mindfulness into existing routines. Even a few minutes of mindful breathing can make a big difference.

Strategies for Overcoming Challenges

Develop a Supportive Routine: Establish a regular mindfulness practice, even if it's just a few minutes a day. Consistency is key to overcoming initial challenges.

Find a Mindfulness Community: Connect with others who are also interested in mindfulness. Sharing experiences and challenges can be motivating and supportive.

Practice Self-Compassion: Be kind to yourself throughout your mindfulness journey. Acknowledge your struggles and celebrate your progress, no matter how small.

Focus on the Benefits: Remind yourself of the positive changes you're experiencing as you cultivate mindfulness. This can help you stay motivated when challenges arise.

Seek Guidance: Consider working with a mindfulness teacher or therapist who can provide personalized support and address specific challenges.

Staying Motivated on your Path

- **Identify Your "Why":** Remind yourself why you started practicing mindfulness in the first place. Is it to reduce stress, improve focus, or cultivate more compassion? Keeping your goals in mind can fuel your motivation.

- **Celebrate Milestones:** Take time to acknowledge your

progress, no matter how small. Did you manage to stay focused for a few extra minutes during meditation? Celebrate these victories!

- **Find Inspiration:** Read books and articles about mindfulness, listen to guided meditations, or watch inspiring talks on the topic. Surrounding yourself with positive influences can keep you motivated.

- **Embrace the Journey:** Mindfulness is a lifelong practice. There will be ups and downs along the way. Embrace the journey, learn from your challenges, and enjoy the process of becoming more present.

Remember: Challenges are an inevitable part of the path to presence. The key is to view them as opportunities for growth and learning. By developing a supportive routine, practicing self-compassion, and staying focused on your "why," you can overcome obstacles and deepen your mindfulness practice. As you cultivate presence, you'll experience a greater sense of peace, well-being, and connection to the present moment.

CHAPTER 13

THE RIPPLE EFFECT: KINDNESS AS THE KEY TO WELL-BEING

Helping others is a win-win. You spread kindness and peace, and seeing the good you do bring a happiness that trophies can't buy. - **Abilasha U R**

In our previous chapters, we explored the power of mindfulness and mental clarity. We learned to cultivate inner peace by taming distractions and quieting our inner critic. But the journey to well-being extends beyond our own minds. True happiness and fulfillment come from connecting with something larger than ourselves – a sense of purpose and connection to others.

This chapter delves into the transformative power of kindness and service. It's not just about feeling good by helping others; it's about understanding the profound impact such actions can have on our own mental and emotional well-being.

Shifting Focus: From "Me" to "We"

Our society often emphasizes competition, achievement, and personal gain. We're constantly bombarded with messages about "getting ahead" and "having it all." While striving for goals is important, the relentless pursuit of self-interest can lead to feelings of isolation, anxiety, and emptiness.

Imagine Sarah, the busy professional we met earlier. Consumed by her demanding job, she spends most of her energy on climbing the corporate ladder. She views colleagues as potential rivals and rarely seeks opportunities to connect or offer help. As a result, Sarah feels isolated and unfulfilled, despite her outward success.

The Science of Kindness

Research overwhelmingly shows the positive impact of kindness on both the giver and receiver. Acts of kindness, big or small, trigger the release of feel-good chemicals like dopamine and oxytocin in the brain. These chemicals promote feelings of happiness, connection, and reduce stress and anxiety.

Kindness isn't just about grand gestures; it's about the everyday choices we make. A simple act of holding the door open for someone, offering a genuine compliment, or volunteering your time can make a significant difference.

The Benefits of Serving Others

Here are some key benefits of incorporating kindness and service into your life:

Reduced Stress and Anxiety: Helping others reduces self-absorption and promotes a sense of purpose. By focusing on the needs of others, we take a break from our own worries and anxieties.

Increased Happiness and Well-being: Acts of kindness trigger the release of feel-good chemicals in the brain, leading to a more positive outlook and overall well-being.

Stronger Relationships: Kindness fosters positive connections with others, building trust and a sense of belonging.

Enhanced Self-Esteem: Helping others can boost your self-worth and create a sense of accomplishment.

Imagine a different scenario for Sarah. She starts incorporating small acts of kindness into her daily routine. She offers to help a colleague with a challenging task, volunteers at a local food bank, and sends a handwritten note of appreciation to her mentor. These acts of service not only benefit others but also contribute to Sarah's own sense of purpose and connection.

Avoiding Nonsense: Cultivating Positive Habits

Our focus shouldn't be on competing with others, gossiping, or engaging in negativity. These "nonsense things" drain our energy and create unnecessary stress. Instead, let's cultivate positive habits that nourish our minds and spirits.

- Practice Gratitude: Take time each day to appreciate the good things in your life, no matter how small. This practice fosters a positive outlook and reduces feelings of negativity.

- Engage in Activities You Enjoy: Make time for activities that bring you joy and a sense of fulfillment. This could be anything from reading to spending time in nature to pursuing a creative hobby.

- Focus on Growth: Embrace learning and development. Take a class, learn a new skill, or simply challenge yourself to try new things. Growth fosters a sense of purpose and keeps the mind engaged.

- Develop Healthy Relationships: Nurture authentic connections with positive and supportive people.

The Ripple Effect: Kindness in Action

Remember, **kindness is contagious.** When we choose to be kind, it inspires others to do the same. This creates a ripple effect, fostering a more positive and compassionate world.

By incorporating service and kindness into your life, you're not just helping others; you're investing in your own mental and emotional well-being.

Embrace the Power of "**We**"

Shifting our focus from **"me" to "we"** is a powerful step towards a happier and more fulfilling life. Kindness isn't a weakness; it's a strength. It's about recognizing our interconnectedness and choosing to contribute to a more positive world. So, go forth and spread kindness! You might be surprised at the positive impact it has on yourself and everyone around you.

CHAPTER 14

PUTTING IT INTO PRACTICE – EXERCISES AND TRACKERS FOR MINDFUL LIVING

"Small steps in mindfulness lead to profound inner peace. Begin today." – **Abilasha U R**

Bonus Chapter: Practical Exercises for Mindfulness and Self-Awareness

As you journey through "Mind Your Own Mind," it's essential to apply what you've learned to your daily life. This bonus chapter offers practical exercises and trackers to help you cultivate mindfulness, self-awareness, and inner peace. Use these tools to integrate the book's teachings into your routine, ensuring lasting change and personal growth.

Daily Mindfulness Exercises

1. Morning Mindfulness Ritual

- *Objective*: Start your day with clarity and calm.

- *Instructions*:

    - Spend 5-10 minutes in silence after waking up.

    - Focus on your breath, observing each inhale and exhale.

    - Set an intention for the day, such as "I will stay present" or "I will be kind to myself."

2. Mindful Eating

- *Objective*: Cultivate awareness during meals.

- *Instructions*:

    - Eat one meal a day without distractions (no phone, TV, or reading).

- Pay attention to the colors, textures, and flavors of your food.

- Chew slowly, savoring each bite.

3. Evening Reflection

- *Objective*: Reflect on your day and identify areas for growth.

- *Instructions*:

  - Spend 5-10 minutes before bed reviewing your day.

  - Ask yourself questions like: "What moments was I fully present?" "When did I feel stressed or distracted?"

  - Write down your thoughts in a journal.

Weekly Self-Awareness Exercises

1. Gratitude Journal

- *Objective*: Foster a positive mindset by acknowledging the good in your life.

- *Instructions*:

  - At the end of each day, write down three things you are grateful for.

  - ◦ Reflect on why these things are meaningful to you.

2. Mindful Walking

- *Objective*: Integrate mindfulness into physical activity.

- *Instructions*:

  - ◦ Take a 20-30 minute walk once a week, focusing on the sensation of your feet on the ground.

  - ◦ Notice your surroundings, paying attention to sights, sounds, and smells.

3. Self-Check-In

- *Objective*: Regularly assess your mental and emotional state.

- *Instructions*:

  - ◦ Set aside 10 minutes each week to check in with yourself.

  - ◦ Ask questions like: "How am I feeling?" "What do I need right now?"

  - ◦ Write down your responses and any action steps.

Monthly Trackers

1. Mindfulness Tracker

- *Objective*: Track your mindfulness practice and progress.

- *Instructions*:

    - Create a calendar with daily slots.

    - Mark each day you practice mindfulness (meditation, mindful eating, etc.).

    - Note any patterns or improvements over the month.

2. Personal Growth Tracker

- *Objective*: Monitor your personal development and achievements.

- *Instructions*:

    - List your goals for the month (e.g., "Practice mindfulness for 10 minutes daily").

    - At the end of each week, reflect on your progress and adjust your goals as needed.

    - Celebrate your achievements and identify areas for further growth.

◦ Reflection and Integration

At the end of each month, take time to reflect on your mindfulness journey. Use the following prompts to guide your reflection:

- **What have I learned about myself this month?**

- **How has mindfulness impacted my daily life?**

- **What challenges did I face, and how did I overcome them?**

- **What are my goals for the next month?**

By consistently practicing these exercises and using the trackers, you'll create a solid foundation for mindfulness and self-awareness. Remember, the journey towards inner peace is ongoing. Embrace each moment and continue to mind your own mind.

CONCLUSION: OWNING YOUR MIND AND EMBRACING THE PRESENT MOMENT

C ongratulations! You've embarked on a journey of self-discovery and explored powerful tools for cultivating a mindful and present life. "Mind Your Own Mind" has equipped you with strategies to:

- **Master your thoughts:** You've learned techniques to tame the wandering mind, overcome negativity, and cultivate a positive mindset.

- **Embrace impermanence:** By accepting the ever-changing nature of life, you've gained resilience and the ability to navigate challenges with greater ease.

- **Practice non-judgment:** Letting go of self-criticism and judgment towards others allows you to experience greater inner peace and foster stronger relationships.

- **Cultivate gratitude:** Shifting your focus to the good things in life fosters a sense of contentment and appreciation for the present moment.

- **Communicate mindfully:** You've learned to connect with others on a deeper level through active listening, empathy, and clear communication.

- **Develop compassion:** By understanding and sharing the suffering of others (and yourself), you've created a foundation for more meaningful connections and a kinder world.

- **Integrate mindfulness:** You've discovered strategies to weave mindfulness into your daily routine, transforming everyday activities into opportunities for present-moment awareness.

Owning Your Mind: A Lifelong Journey

Remember, "Mind Your Own Mind" is just the beginning. Mindfulness and self-mastery are lifelong journeys. Continue to explore, experiment with different techniques, and find what works best for you. As you cultivate these practices, you'll experience a profound shift in your inner world:

Reduced Stress and Anxiety: By managing your thoughts and accepting the present moment, you'll find greater inner peace and calmness.

Enhanced Well-being: Mindfulness fosters greater self-compassion, stronger relationships, and a deeper appreciation for life, leading to overall well-being.

Increased Focus and Productivity: Taming your wandering mind allows you to focus more effectively and achieve your goals with greater clarity.

Greater Purpose and Connection: Living with presence allows you to connect with yourself and others on a deeper level, fostering a sense of purpose and fulfillment.

Embrace the Present Moment

The present moment is the only thing you truly have. By "Minding Your Own Mind" and cultivating mindfulness, you can transform your present experiences, build a more fulfilling future, and create a life filled with peace, purpose, and connection.

Go forth, own your mind, and embrace the wonder of the present moment!

All the best.

DISCLAIMER

This book is for educational purposes only. Readers acknowledge that the author does not render legal, financial, medical, or professional advice. The content within this book has been derived from various sources. Please consult a licensed professional before attempting any techniques outlined in this book.

By reading this document, the reader agrees that under no circumstances is the author responsible for any direct or indirect losses incurred as a result of the use of the information contained within this document, including but not limited to errors, omissions, or inaccuracies.

Adherence to all applicable laws and regulations, including international, federal, state, and local governing professional licensing, business practices, advertising, and all other jurisdictions, is the sole responsibility of the purchaser or reader.

Neither the author nor the publisher assumes any responsibility or liability whatsoever on behalf of the purchaser or reader of these materials. Any perceived slight of any individual or organization is purely unintentional.